The Word

KINGDOM

in the Word

KINGDOM

Also by Noah Eli Gordon

Books

The Frequencies
(Tougher Disguises, 2003)

The Area of Sound Called the Subtone
(Ahsahta Press, 2004)

Inbox
(BlazeVox, 2006)

A Fiddle Pulled from the Throat of a Sparrow
(New Issues, 2007)

Novel Pictorial Noise
(Harper Perennial, 2007)

Figures for a Darkroom Voice
(Tarpaulin Sky Press, 2007; with Joshua Marie Wilkinson)

The Source
(Futurepoem Books, 2011)

The Year of The Rooster
(Ahsahta Press, 2013)

Chapbooks and Limited Edition Pamphlets

The Fire & The Blue, Ten Frequencies, A Falling in Autumn, The Neat Life of Nicely-Nicely Lincoln, The Laughing Alphabet, Untitled Essays, Notes Toward the Spectacle, Jaywalking the Is, What Ever Belongs in the Circle, How Human Nouns, That We Come to a Consensus, Twenty Ruptured Paragraphs from a Perfectly Functional Book, A New Hymn to the Old Night, Flag, Returning Diminishments, Acoustic Experience, Three Spider Stories, Fifteen Problems.

The Word

KINGDOM

in the Word

KINGDOM

Noah Eli Gordon

Brooklyn Arts Press · New York

The Word *Kingdom* in the Word Kingdom
© 2015 Noah Eli Gordon

ISBN-13: 978-1-936767-38-0

Cover design by David Drummond. Interior design by Joe Pan &
Noah Eli Gordon. Back cover author drawing by Zachary Schomburg.

Published in the United States of America by:
Brooklyn Arts Press
154 N 9th St #1
Brooklyn, NY 11249
WWW.BROOKLYNARTSPRESS.COM
INFO@BROOKLYNARTSPRESS.COM

Distributed to the trade by Small Press Distribution (SPD)
spdbooks.org

Library of Congress Cataloging-in-Publication Data

Gordon, Noah Eli, 1975-
[Poems. Selections]
The word kingdom in the word kingdom / Noah Eli Gordon.
    pages ; cm
ISBN 978-1-936767-38-0 (pbk. : alk. paper)
I. Title.
PS3607.O5943A6 2014
811'.6--dc23
                                2014019665

10 9 8 7 6 5 4 3 2 1
FIRST EDITION

CONTENTS

1

2

3

_____

acknowledgments

for Sommer & Georgia

The Word

KINGDOM

in the Word

KINGDOM

A crown lies / under the cake.

—Barbara Guest

1

AN EXAMPLE

A subway car
passes through the room
in which I'm discussing
examples of enjambment
with several poets. We talk
about these lines by Schuyler:

A gray hush
in which the boxy trucks roll up Second Avenue
into the sky. They're just
going over the hill.

No, it's not a subway
car. It's simply the windows

of a subway car, positioned
precisely where they'd be

were they
attached

to a subway car. I point
in the direction

the windows, for all
we know, are

still headed, say
there's
my example.

FOR EXPRESSION

Sing a song of utterance. I mutter to you.
Sing a song of expression.
—Gertrude Stein

For the feel
  in my palm
  of an apple
  fresh from
  the market
Against the
  viscous
  transparent skin
  of marketing

For the condition
  of air
Against air
  conditioning

For the brightness
  of the room made
  brighter by an
  illuminating act
  of the imagination
Against ingredients
  and blueprints

For the continued sweetness
  of chilled plums
Against plumage

Against the rifles
  the aggressors
  of elegant discourse
  display as flags
For riffling elegantly
  through discourse
  to display
  aggression flagging

For the curve
  of any Adonis's cock
Against a lecture
  on how to cup
  the sack while stroking

For the renewal
  of sunsets and moons
  seasons tiny saplings
  soups of all kinds
Against novelty
  stirring in the wrong direction

For patronage
Against patrons

For music
Against museums

For the body
  in its folds
  and dignities
Against collapsing
  garment factories

For love
Against labels

For workers
Against force

For the mask's respect
  of the contours
  of the human face
Against hanging it
  on a wall
  backwards

For paintings
Against frames

For pleasure
Against its conscription
  to a purely cerebral
  paradise

For standing
  however
  you see fit
Against posturing

For buildings
Against scaffolding

For the suit
Against the numbers

For the public
Against the publicist

For the sudden sharp beauty
  of seeing anew
  again
  the same
  old world
Against the art
  of money
  the artifact

the art of facts
and administration

For water
  that rises and falls
  the earth
  those on it
Against the pull
  of the village
  explainer

For weather
Against forecasts

For the cow
Against the brand

For Stein and Césaire
  Vallejo
  Sappho Rimbaud
Against Cage and Warhol
  Google
  Apple
  Monsanto

For the capacity
  to imagine
  your nakedness

Against endless images
    of it

For the thread
Against the mill

For the attendant enchantment
    of a phrase
    tuned
    and trued
Against taking attendance

For enchantment
    in general
Against the generals
    of entrenched
    imagination

For the clit
Against the clock

For poles and zones
Against polling and zoning

For plasticity
Against plastic

For the poets
  grown old
  before us
Against their mistaking
  admiration
  for eros

For a wooden door
  painted green
  impervious
  to weather
Against whether
  or not
  one has
  to open it

For options
Against operators

For photographs
  of flowers
  all over the place
Against poems
  where people
  aim telephoto lenses
  at one another

For pushing
    the last bits
    of daylight
    through
    the door locks
Against polishing
    your crown
    behind the curtains

For a girl
    floating
    for a few seconds
    across
    the parking lot
Against what's only
    an ordinary
    skateboard
    underneath her

For the desire
    to walk around
    and around the block
    like a man who takes
    pleasure
    in circling something
    he knows he won't

apply for because
he's certain he'd get it
Against applications

For another poem
   textured
   with the sky
   night
   stars
   and the sun
Against its textual history

For the messianic
   and
Against the messianic
   and
For the freedom to be so
   and
Against the fastidiousness not to

HISTORICAL CRITICISM AND THE IMAGE OF THE HEART

Its beating was always allegorical. One hears it
in a scene where someone crouches
behind something, or in the subbasement
of one's own response to what the day, stumbling in
at an odd hour, strews across the bedroom floor.
Isn't fashion last year's scandal declawed?
The books we'd loved best told us on every page
to wake, whether to hunger, cannon fire,
or the warmth of another's body. As for painting,
its greatest achievements, of which you know
I'm no authority, are replicated in
wrinkled sheets. By *you*, I mean the both of us.
A new focal point brings the promise
of finally seeing for the first time what we'd been
looking at all along: sunsets. Then photographs
of sunsets. Then better photographs of sunsets.
Then perfect digital copies. Then computerized
reenactments. Then, simply, ones and zeros.

ON DISMANTLING CLASSICAL VOCABULARY

Two tragedies occur simultaneously
A hummingbird coming apart in thin sun
is neither first nor the second one
Hear morning recast in sound
the body's trace symmetry
When is the age of analysis not upon us
its orange curtains filtering
twice the sun & twice
the sentence from which sun falls
The difficulty of replicating darkness
too much blue around the black earth
too many binaries making uncomfortable beds
Goodnight air full of astronauts
There is no tree. There is no modernism

WHAT DO I KNOW

for Michael Burkard

I was going to read your new book tonight going to start
on the balcony where I go to smoke standing next
to a square of light let out by the little window there
which gives enough to see if all the apartment lights are on
since I still haven't changed the bulb above the porch a waste
I know I was going to read but the snow was too strong
it blew right into the first few pages so I closed the book
and smoked with my back to the wind which felt
deliberate and defiant at the same time I mean the act
not the weather although I know either way works really
ten years ago I wrote "gushing self-pity" next to a poem
in one of your books I'm sorry ten years ago I thought I knew
everything about what poems should do now I know I know
very little and that it's better this way standing here in the dark

GEPPETTO ALSO MADE A MOTHER

for Michael Friedman

There is nothing imaginary
about a piece of wood.
It has its life, like you
or I, and returns to the ocean.
Gravity won't allow the wheel to roll
up a hill. Having no imagination, a piece
of wood doesn't care
if it becomes a fan blade,
a coffee table, or a little wheel
on a wooden horse. Real marionettes
have no strings. Real horses, arriving
at hills, may or may not climb them.
This has nothing to do
with free will, an invention
of purely academic interest.
The Chinese invented stirrups,
and their hills have been covered
with horses ever since.
On a clear day, the ocean goes on
forever. Like Oedipus alone
on a hilltop, this is a literary device
used to demonstrate the value

of beachfront property. Italian
literature has never had room
for gravity. Like you or I, it has
its life, returning always to the ocean.
It doesn't care if it becomes something
to cover a coffee table.
Strings pull real wooden horses.
This is an example of the imposition
of free will on inanimate objects.
There is nothing imaginary
about the historic importance
of the stirrup's role.
On a clear day, it is possible
to see wooden storks
clouding the air.

A THEORY OF THE NOVEL

Something miraculous

springs from the next sentence, but already
you'd skimmed to the end.

***

A boy's attention, corralled
in sand, pebbles, and the sun's
slow clockwork, fails

to take in

the wreckage, though
years from now, he'll

describe it perfectly.

***

So will you.

THE WORD *KINGDOM*
IN THE WORD KINGDOM

for Julie Carr & Tim Roberts

An eleven-year-old's inability to find Eden on a map

returns the word *kingdom* to the Word Kingdom, where the end

of history, with its tail in its mouth, talks back to St. Augustine

in antiquated sign language. The sign for a second river.

Instance. Another second river. Sign for a concrete universal

byproduct, for virtual models of interesting parts

of the earth. Sign for endangered species, for endemic

spectacles. Sign for the question: And then who went down

to the ship? And who stood in the bluest spot of a green field

in a white shirt and whittled futility at passing airplanes?

A bad gambler in the abstract makes a good Samaritan

imprisoned in her own activity. Now, the seven-year-old

tells her brother the door he's labeled *Nowhere* can't be there.

The speaker at the computer isn't silent. It's silence.

In the Word Kingdom, the sad human *you*, theoretical

as money, pushes its toy train in saintly straight lines.

Pray for an ark full of adverbs dissolving midair and ungoing

grammar's perennial it leaves tracks. They're yours, your tracks.

Your causality. Your tautological cabin in the woods

hermetically aflame with the coldest of fires. The best way

to describe a forest is to run from it. The best arrows are

aimless, egolessly yielding to air, bent into age, broken on badges.

Reject multitudes. Eject pilots. Jettison the cargo bay. There there,

persistent soliloquy of a present inexorably diffuse. Fox in

the sewer. Face in wood grain. A fish with a name. A crow's chorus

of *me me me* replacing the word *kingdom* in the Word Kingdom

with ants and their *us* makes noise in the new realism

picture a story and point once upon again this time.

Tell me the once upon a time again—picture of a story

pointing to the universe. Halfway between halfway between.

Or picture a story and point. The universe is everywhere

authoritatively. Each *that that that* the baby names:

little embraced idea—our resplendent lacuna grown larger.

As though nodding in utter agreement udder's bereavement,

every child falls down a well, father in tow. Same well.

Same story's indifference. Same day moon in winter sun

above an island of garbage. Every desire, aiming in the same

direction. Every direction, aimless. Every aim, directionless.

Odysseus to Olive Oyl and Popeye to Penelope. Dust to plastic

and love's digital reenactment. If I think of rain I think of rain,

but that doesn't mean it does. That *that* that Word Kingdom wants

wants us to write a room full of it, umbilically delinquent.

First, there was a picture without its spectator, then the world

bursting with spring. Curbstone. Gravestone. A cradle's throne.

First there were pigeons, then the sky fell. Now, for a dollar

they'll take your picture on this pony. Or better, for five

you can ride. Loving names and their lovely arrogance

mimicked in swaddling clothes. In the Word Kingdom

the word *kingdom* can't straddle its horse. It doesn't have one.

There are no animals there. No currycombs, stirrups, saddles.

No bridles or yokes. No *A* for antelope. *O* for oxen refusing

to be aimed. Wake to the Word Kingdom sawing its legs

to fit the iron bed, then look at how light hits this desk perfectly

and leave it there. It's the only map to Eden, which is only a map.

Tissue paper to body tissue issuing a bracelet for the wrist

as a house for the guest is a dead bee in the light bulb dumb as any.

BEST AMERICAN
EXPERIMENTAL POETRY

1.

Aristotle divided pleasure
into two kinds: necessary
physical pleasures and those
that are good and pleasant
that we desire but don't need

2.

At twenty, I couldn't believe
the vodka they had
at this party was a top-notch
brand, that they were just giving it
away, the best thing I'd then
tasted, until someone came
ever so carefully to refill
the fancy bottles with cheap stuff

3.

If pressed, my nineteen-month-old daughter
can count to three. But after two, she prefers
to start over

POEM FOR NEDĀ ĀGHĀ-SOLTĀN

but for a bird's pursuit of specifics

specific bird vague pursuit

  vanitas

but for egrets in elms on old newspaper

Iranian videos in the age of vellum

the isotropic werkglocken's
    decorous continuity errors
erecting the abiding pleasure which gardens confer

      vagrant history
asleep in the tub, a slip of the tongue

paper talking truculence

    but for the sky   sky   sky

    mother me reluctant I's adjective

what egret yesterday's p-p-pixel

now, tomorrow's unlidded eye
adopts that toward which it steers:

    the problem of the camera
    answering its kingme in triplicate—

no synonym
for the sadness
of a Nebraskan miller moth's
postcoital death in Denver

June's June looks out from largesse—

a votive battleship's feet in the sand

later misunderstandings

    of recent date

recline around the flame

    as though a poem

pitched to the moon

    with no astronaut in it

accounts for past tense, tenuous

so much of muck
to mulch a boy
imagining a tree house
and living there a week
for an hour

the dead girl alive

deadlive enemy of kinship crow's-nest

newspaper aflame in love with the front porch
like music that wants you only, only to know it's music

only specifics   only moths

only 300 Wednesdays in memoriam

but for the long pale door
to the lawn, which is not
anthemic location, but an afternoon
I waste tracing a microphone
on tiny Post-it notes

proof of the dead girl's living pursuant

seeing that that have not seen thy face

WHY I AM NOT AN ACADEMIC

There's the sun

And there—
        the culture of sun

The first word spoken
in its shadow
was a verb

The first spoken in the shadow
        of its shadow
        an adjective

One dances
        to decorous music

The other
        hardly moves at all

EARTHLY SITUATION

If I could just get that finch in that tree on this day perfectly

pinned the flat world let fly pilgrim-like from the podium

not to say *I was here* but here I stay a photograph of the photographer

facing grace but a body looking elsewhere to us believe it or

just say *tree* so lush the world rushes if I could just get that

you were, are, there, here—too many cars, kids, cats, scented candles

Too much ephemera. Exasperation

Archival as the cruise ship locker where they keep the rocking chairs

If I could just can't be leisure, can't be leashed to distant higher ends—

dog whining for outdoors the day day's gotten in the way of itself again

Not that final meeting
In the twilight kingdom

—T.S. Eliot

2

TEN WAYS TO PUT TOGETHER AN AIRPLANE

1.

Turn toward the undifferentiated vastness in the first of all flowers.

2.

Turn partly in delight & partly inspired by the sick awe of rebirth.

3.

Turn a weakness of the libido into the asset of a well-stocked garage.

4.

Shatter utopian tendencies against the earthly ballast that anchors them.

5.

Turn a spiritual aspiration into the ill-omened echo of a dog's far-off cry.

6.

Turn animals into theologians, psychotherapists, classicists, & art critics.

7.

This theory would liken flight to a kind of castration of the intellect.

8.

Engage in nothing on the fringe of everyday activities save that of
    forgetfulness.

9.

Turn the sonnet like a saw blade upon the woodsy fixity of received form.

10.

Launch into the air an asexual organ of reproduction. Say it: fuel equals fear.

AN EXPERIMENT IN ARTIFICE AND ABJECT-ORIENTED ONTOLOGY

between a prayer for the telescope

and a prayer for the microscope

pixels flare into the image of an atom

in an anthill an airplane entering

the troposphere an idea orbiting

that of human cognition in the authoritative

shape of earth seen from elsewhere

antiquating the twentieth century's

representational doubt or doubting

representations of ownership

in our condensed book of vigilance

where the absence of a crown

shows hierarchy to have no color

I prefer the muddy ghost of one

sustained cello note over one

hundred thousand science experiments

I prefer two electrified balloons

pushing away from each other

like localized points of reference

perhaps one can love the academic sentence

for its ethical contortions the footnote

for its fishhooks pulling up islands

from an ocean floor perhaps a barge

passing below a bridge exemplifies

a green horizon free from the expectation

of green blackened with carbon completely

submerged the egg holds around it

a fine film of air it is silver the silver

of barges and the silver of bridges

a perfect pear-shaped lampshade

bringing to the room an understanding

of artifice the silver shape of Colorado

in spring its glossy parody of an ideal

landscape shattered by the airplane window

crossed out like the X wedged into

a representation of the upper atmosphere

the sun's light is white this is the light

of example a world within a red lampshade

whose idea of orange is a tiny dandelion

giving to a field its greenness anyone

can bend and scatter blue and violet rays

but who puts together a life by praising

mathematical air around an elephant

half of the sky excuses itself

from such a question sixty-five million

years ago an asteroid smashed into

the earth what remains is loneliness

for the nihilistic imperative withdrawn

as Copernicus withered as an oak leaf

clinging like an aura of classical inevitability

around the little effort it takes to imagine

a scorpion you don't admire an icon you

just click on it the airplane and the

atmosphere were never one spiraling

through a pre-Mayan zero's impossible

boundary the barge and the bridge were

never one a seed disintegrates in soil

complete potentiality comes to the elephant

and the egg one validates the other's

annulment reaching toward the lamp

someone's decided the world's too full

of illumination both captain and pilot

survive scrutiny as the barge destroys

the view from the bridge and the

nomenclature of clouds gives the day

another creation myth to ignore the guts

of a piano would make a good example

but of what I'm unsure so we continue

to engineer our architectural music

taking cues from Chaucer like clues

from the hourglass shape of a Chinese

alchemist's furnace too much symbolism

annihilates the sublimated form therefore

no one mentions swans anymore would you

rather have a goddess of terror

to whom goats are sacrificed or

the implications of Eve signifying human

sensitivity entrenched in the post-

European psyche for another millennium

I'm through thinking in images says

the bodily eye to its narrative

dismemberment while a decapitated head

rolls out of the cliché and I've built

another victim of fully embodied rhetoric

and in this lies the difference between

picture and proposition between

thinking afresh as if nothing had happened

and taking a tidal wave apart a salty

phoneme sinks in sand it is not

novel pictorial noise but the limits

of draftsmanship standing for the limits

of earthly existence removed from

the videocassette multi-petaled rose-like

I give you permission to see beneath

the apparent image of the flower

in this model two prongs of a fork

are pushed into a cork J'Lyn moves

from Joshua Paul and Kristin expand

without tipping or toppling over the fern

marks an absolute conclusion simplistic

and perishable impermanence yes

the gymnast considers another balancing

experiment and our boat demonstrates

a failure to parse the greenest of sentences

the fork however is easily returned

to the drawer the fern to the forest

airplane to the air and the elephant

to the twisted nucleotides that give it order

after the piano was repaired its music

seemed dated derivative as attention

tossed to the ruptured balloon ruining

the experiment's proof of repulsion

but proving sideways listening a kind

of detonation a miniature electric cell

in which notes are to noise as bees

are to a shaft of wheat compressed

into the best tasting bread things don't

correspond they coalesce a lion crushes

a dandelion a crown crushes abstract

autonomy Dante damns his enemies

in every new translation as true images

are collapsing again into the earth

we enter the Clouds of Magellan

only to drift like heterogeneous ideas

yoked together by violets this is

the terrible loneliness of an electron's

orbit botany and pornography fused

into the most aerodynamic of asteroids

goodbye Hegelian aliens the rational alone

is a real hinge pulpy and puffy children

swing in summertime alive as animation

so much for the playground hypothesis

of a disaster movie ripping open

an already cauterized cultural wound

you like novels and I like nudity

underneath all utilitarian and decorative states

an instrument of epiphany sits unstrung

as a book of etiquette from the age

of cause and effect American acoustics

thrive in their theatrical qualities

while the sky drained of any significance

drops like a curtain over our embrace

of reading into the empirical now

the piano implicates us in its generous

and possessive melody the cricket emerges

an imago parents roam from room

to room demolishing themselves

like Socratic students both egg

and airplane crack leaving no other trace

than the transitory and arbitrary volume

of a little air tender wreckage

grass nailed objectively to the ground

QUESTIONS FOR
FURTHER STUDY

The guts of a piano
exemplify uncertainty
beneath the apparent image
of fully embodied rhetoric, but how
can one talk about music
without destroying it?
Muddy at midday, the ghost
of one sustained cello note
mirrors an elephant's
mathematical air, but what
does scale matter to the dead?
It takes little effort to imagine
a dandelion, little more
to bend it, but how is effort little?
How does a seed contort potentiality?
What's novel about twisted nucleotides?
Why are the best questions
miniature copies of massive doubts?
Is the swan still an empty symbol?
Can a poem really take an airplane apart?

TEN WAYS TO TAKE
AN AIRPLANE APART

1

A rivet forces
two sheets
of aluminum
into proximity

Violence to the hawk and violence
to the horse, together, build
a third kind of animal. Wholly subdued, hanger-like

This tangential harmony—impossible
as a mountain in the ant's understanding
of an airfield. Nothing's joined
that wasn't broken from itself
thus, the sexual elevator
crushes a man holding
a bouquet of lilies

An orchid lashed to a tree
proves original theory untenable

Is this how you underline
your way into the pantheon

Pegasus was a horse. The airplane
an automobile. A pillow
for earth-bound egos purified
in upper air. Orgasm tears the plane apart

2

Was it a flock of black helicopters
I mistook for an early turn of evening

Interrogation's a landing pad in a garden
A tiny X hovering over the question

what variable doesn't love wilting

The only thing that pulls a fly
from the air is exhaustion

Grounded by a noisy ionosphere
cut in half by a cloud, adrift
in the concussive intermingling
of imagined things, my desire remains
the same: explode the word "construct"

3

I give you
the undisturbed image
of the airplane

then a sun
tied to the sky
by schematics

like a crayon
crushed on a blackboard

an interrogative parachute
in pastels on dyed paper

implicit as a doorway in the dark
or poor Ophelia's waterlogged dress

enough gravelly syllables
to lay a runway
in any conceivable language

your refusal to land
turning away
from the rhetorical

4

If mutual agreement explains the world
is that ladybug example or arithmetic

Dear apple, the earth photographed
in its entirety doesn't place you

at odds with your animal
That's perspective's job

Nude awareness is nothing new
Who says a cockpit can't be comfortable

Automation never found a gardener
in want of work, but seeding the clouds

above this mechanical sense
of draftsmanship begs the question

is it still impossible to improve
upon the ladder

I plant my little doubts and people like little dots
can't assemble the airplane from this distance

5

a painter hacks apart an explanation of the yellow jacket

the first step of a descent down the airplane

a relative ladder and yet a ladder

an alloy of zinc and aluminum

cast into the shape of contingency

a geometric plane perhaps

or perhaps a pipe cleaner twisted into a plane

another miniature trope

to model full-scale diminishments of full-scale expansions

an opaque airfoil pantomime

the expansive inauguration of which

the inchoately described decomposition of a wing

after all is the ladder at the end of the airplane

or else its attempt to reach an actual cloud

6 (dissolving aphorisms for a skywriter)

The history of human ingenuity has a somber disregard for the genuinely human.

With every mention of Icarus, the house of buoyant particulars rocks a little on its foundation.

A bird goes to great lengths to construct its nest before knowing there are such things as eggs, but what architect isn't born disregarding?

Building is the most beautiful verb.

It is without language that our bird is perched on a branch of the word *tree* imagining a grammar flightless.

The airplane's animal image is artificial.

7

The airplane is a metaphor
of annulment, a body
whose borders are flayed, districts redrawn
to allow their constituents
election of infinite stillness
for the engine's interior, a platform
upon which a butchered animal's organs
are to a system for organizing experience
as an air traffic controller's contortions
are to the weather wedged within a keyhole
which is to say once you open a thing
return is impossible. A door closes
A day closes. Eggs plummet to the earth
as the ant ignores the orchid
and both go on eating their air

8

If an annulment of metaphor
is negation's landing gear, and contiguity
gives the ambulance its atmosphere
of maudlin frenzy, what colored siren
would smash its medicine against the rocks

Take a few minutes to formulate a response

In the meantime, the question begins its turbulent descent

And afterwards? Afterwards

9

The problem of the airplane is falling. Obscure and groundless chronology agitates its origins, asserting that the problem of the airplane is falling from a paragraph, from a pair of graphs etched on an apple after it too is bruised by correspondence, forced to stand an aggregate for aviation, subjugated by painting, and slipped into a pocket like an icon condensed into a diacritical mark.

So the airplane's century receives its music in microtonal intervals. Flowers break apart. Elevators drift like outlines controlled to an almost infinite degree, a result of improvisation. After its dismemberment, the falling problem of the airplane fails to put a yellow jacket back together. Listen, decibels don't measure sound; they destroy it.

10

The ideal
airplane
is paper

Crush it
in your
palm

slow
the sound
a thousand-fold

hear
a violet
opening

AN OLD POEM EMBEDDED IN A FINAL THOUGHT ON THE AIRPLANE

About fifteen years ago, I wrote a short poem called "Yesterday I Named a Dead Bird Rebecca." The title came to me while in Florida visiting family. Going for a short walk, I passed the carcass of a crow swarming with small flies. There was something so repugnant about this particular dead animal that, although oddly aware of its lack of any sort of odor, I was, nonetheless, overcome by a strong, debilitating nausea, one which I suspect arose simply from the smell I imagined the bird to have. The poem reads:

> were a defused heart
> wintering the clock
>
> time kept
> by counting birds
>
> I'd call flight
> a half-belief in air
>
> a venomous lack
> when the ticking is less so

What could be more obvious than that this poem transposes its propositional way of understanding gravity into the structure of its own identity? Something that lies beyond the purview of its lone sentence speaks to me now as the kind of nostalgia one feels upon watching an airplane pass overhead. It means making distance disappear.

not a word the
mellow stillness
of the sounds are

—Joseph Ceravolo

3

CONTINUED ETHICAL ENGAGEMENT OF THE NARRATIVE TRADITION

Concise articulation wasn't what we'd wanted, exactly.
I'm not so sure the line matters. I'm not so sure
the line matters. You don't just get on a motorcycle and become
a kind of historical category. First, they considered founding
a unified artistic school with a coherent program. Then, the sun
again disappeared over hilltops. Was this the extension of power
by an expansionist idea about the world being purely internalized?
Think: childhood but with the irony, an unattainable condition
in which we collectively float. It takes at least as much scrutiny
as standing on one shore and looking at another. Instead, we spend
a lot of time staring at ink stains. Call it disregard for whatever
one proposes as the latest craze of substantive adherence
and simplistic acquiescence to wallpaper wallpaper wallpaper.
Look imaginatively at a pineapple and disappear. Look imaginatively
at a pineapple and disappear. The poem isn't interested in helping you.

BEST AMERICAN
EXPERIMENTAL POETRY

In last season's
      dust

    burning off

you can't smell
the oily fingerprints

      of whomever
      positioned
      the spotlight

but you can
    amazingly
      see   the power cord

plugged only into itself

EIGHT MEDITATIONS ON ENORMITY, PETRIFACTION, AND WORK

1

Whatever deities have taken up residence in prayer aimed at labor's aftermath won't explain the establishment of a sedentary society, especially one already weighed down with Gospel accounts of bread turned to stone, splinters tumbling from the sky, and pieces of the heavenly throne scattered across our own backyards. I'm pretty sure mystery is simply a privileging of what's not directly in front of one's face. That that which between method and doctrine manifests itself in the decision to finally clean out the sink, restock the cupboard, and make those few remaining phone calls is proof of the tightened apogee of the possible proves there is no difference between one for whom work is freed from acrimonious entanglements and one for whom entanglement works to free acrimony from its surfacing in such daily banality. I'm pretty sure there's nothing mysterious in that.

2

But wasn't there much left to learn from the old ways? Hadn't we heard a literal train of thought approaching from the past? Its pervasive melancholic rumble, partly audible, registering as a vibratory feeling, a taking in of distant movement as one might take in a stray cat, living with it for years, until it too moves on. Isn't ownership questionable? I suppose the certainty of a train's arrival would allow us a little departure, failing that, at least the story would, as they say, grow legs. Awkwardness is part of its appeal, part of what strikes one, for no apparent reason, or for a reason whose appearance is still unjustified, suddenly and completely to accept the first excuse given as the answer one was after all along.

3

It's not resignation, rather a way to effectively seat one's self in the lone remaining chair, nodding toward the left or right, so that for an instant the other passengers regret not having taken a clearly desirable spot. Perhaps I'm not much inclined to venture further than my own comfort can stretch, as though giving up the unknown for larger, headier complications were akin to cataloging the minor advances each day allows, until even these are as easily forgotten as a list of chores accomplished months ago, yet discovered this afternoon, underneath whatever the surface of the desk deemed more important, or at least more pressing. A reclining detail relaxes in redundancy.

4

That a train arrives at all is a small miracle of dependence, a smaller one of reliability. There's weather to anchor us to one another. I mention this hoping you'll agree, and so we're indentured to the startling anecdotes that chisel the face we think we've put on from the lumpy air of individuality surrounding our sense of how the world looks from someone else's perspective. By chance a drop of water lands precisely between coat collar and a bit of exposed neck, almost as a means to further punctuate this point, which, of course, is not random, but another of the mysterious jokes the universe seems to be silently playing, refusing to give itself away with even the slightest of chuckles. It's held in, neither expanding nor dissipating, like a painting of a man puttering around his rooms, another of him picking up or putting down a few treasured objects—scissors, an onyx paperweight, the skull of a monkey with three teeth attached. Is he really turning them over in a way that shows him to be alone with the act? One might claim a kinship with the palette, burn the canvas, and hang the brush on a museum wall.

5

Observation is change. Change is violence. Violence is inevitable. There's no other way to see it. Even a pet is unaware of her owner's eventual return. Music drifts from a window and you're back to the first time you'd heard it. Don't expect this to work for the intervening moments; they're better left to the rubbish heap of accustomed and unobtrusive activity. Here, I think the station's swell of newly quickening passengers means we're primed for another exodus. One would do well to propose an analogy between these momentary surges and those of live electrical currents, not that it would reveal anything novel about the situation, which, in its drab, mundane state, is the operative candidate for a shock or two. It would, however, work as a kind of counter-example, laying siege to the universality of our more entrenched ideas. To paint the word *lighthouse* on a lighthouse is deserving of shipwreck.

6

Don't you want the weight of the thought to have a literal heft, an equivalency you might wear as though it were a shawl, casually, yet calculatingly so. It's not enough to cover the shoulders. This is easy, and ease has its way of undermining the best of plans. Better to scale the walls before thinking of anything approaching an embodiment of the underworld, let alone the nobility that gives it like a blind guard dog its distance. What mythology doesn't have evidence of a gate somewhere at its center? I, for one, am open to reconsidering the usefulness of so flimsy a proposition. As is the case with past action charged with the memory of now unalterable, alternative choice, any nostalgic longing for a tree over the table it's become must take into account every last meal eaten upon it.

7

History has a way of waking us up, not to some bright future, where the telephone rings at the precise moment you were beginning to feel the first pings of loneliness. No, one is woken in a haze, feeling the disorientation of a child mistaking a stranger's dangling arm for that of his mother's. This is the sort of moment out of which entire gardens are planned. Were it not for the invention of clocks and the boarding of factory windows, we would have left work at dusk, dawdled in idle conversation, and been back home in no time. It's true, you can refute the historic role of a stone by simply kicking it.

8

As Prometheus would have it, a human redolence
retained in raw stone descends from heaven
only to rise again above the earth.
Don't delude yourself lifting a tool upon lofty thinking akin to pollution.
Four noble truths. Four feet in a single state. Poor prize-less fourth place
and the upright mammal's interest in purity pulverized
as a white painting of a white lake awash in late office light.
To undertake an economic pilgrimage. To tie feathers to your hair.
Swimming in moral instruction, Chinese peace and Hindu tranquility,
the first original American's redemptive breath: oratorio on top of old smoky.
All outward signs disappear. All disappearances
sign sing scorching O spaciousness!
O death knell conscript chalking walls!
How do I know sexual laxity from the perfect image of self-control?
How do I know an ember from an embryonic dark horse?
Unlikely candidate unlike a future model for town square
smashing a textile machine to deify archeological evidence.
And thusly the Luddite begins anew, as Prometheus would
have it, to retain a human redolence in raw stone
descending from heaven and rising again above the earth.

THE LAUGHING ALPHABET

This is my memory

          of the form of fox: that I was lost as in a boat with oiled gauges & oil lamps, veering, a vexed to-fro left by an impossible wake on the line of water rendered with a blue crayon & lacking depth. The fox crosses a threshold & establishes congruency. The edge of an environment & also an imaginary pain scale. The impulse below a choice that one has where an ideograph will embrace our animal other. So we are entered in the *Guestbook of Boundaries*, where the margins of a page & the pads of each paw, in appearance & atmosphere, void, like a white tourniquet, the stratum cast as a theoretical ax in the actual air.

The form of fox

                       which wounds in moving from our roles
lines of negation, unwritten words, an actor's empty mouth
& also the age of trees. The spark that ignites the form of
fox as ineffable: the shouting of timber & that of tallyho,
the twisting of tarred yard into cordage. A crayon containing
a house, seascape & an infinite edge of forest, where blue
leaves & blue bark influence the translucence the house
that I was lost in looking at takes on & also the water & the
number three.

This is my memory

          of form as that which suffers light
when information is passed from edge to outline, where fox
procedure congeals in selective inspiration: the craft of fox
& also the crafty fox. The intellect that will arrange a boat
& intellectualism's buoyancy. A fox intelligence placing us
outside the frame, a master/student dynamic & the full use
of the page marking one as intelligent. The number seven
on a scale & also its opposite, anti-shadow, equation, Libra
& libretto, a ballroom dance & the broken gait of a mare,
flowering spikes, refuge from enemy fire, phosphorescence,
the use of gloves subsequent to discoloration, the gauges
& generators assumed to belong though absent from the
surface, a formlessness taken on when the fox moves from
the blue forest.

LUGGAGE ARRIVES IN THE WORLD WHERE IT WAITS

for Oren Silverman

just as two lines arrive in the poem as a couplet
so two policemen arrive at the edge of the world

one in front of the other but from a different angle
simply parallel proving authority's only the arrival

of an imposition imposing its rule on whomever
allows the flower to wilt in the tiny world of its water glass

what is the image of happiness if not when
alarms ring out in the world & we ignore them

all the police aimlessly wandering through our poems
the sad pride of all the police aimlessly wandering

how wonderful to sit here and hum
purposefully alive with the fires of boredom

ARS POETICA

Where we are is in a sentence.
—Jack Spicer

Sound out of air, music

out of oak, deeply moved

by meaning, deleting each detail

and the day caves, becomes

ingratiatingly calm, the unwitting

captivity of interruption, evidence

working like a celebrity before stardom.

A MIDNIGHT VILLANELLE

The old villanelle & the young villanelle
smashed together collectively solve the problem
of separation & collision, emptying the cell

of its nucleus, as I have emptied your inkwell
of ink & half-formed words, which the sum
of the old villanelle & the young villanelle

fails to negate yet in failing fails rather well
The old villanelle: "I shall hide the golden plum
of separation & collision, emptying the cell

in which you have caged me, so fare-thee-well
young villanelle. Soon you too will become
the old villanelle." & the young villanelle:

"Just as a red cloud in a white cup impels
one to paint the sky in reverse, so I too succumb
to separation & collision, emptying the cell

in a cyclotron, tearing the door from its bell."
The microscope builds its candescent lies from
the old villanelle & the young villanelle
separating, colliding, emptying the cell

PALATIAL IS THE COMPASS THAT SHALL USHER US IN

Approximated in charcoal on paper
thin as drizzle on a marathon, you want description
to be molting, animalesque—a mandate
counting down to perplexity
Acquiesce to joy!
The blue jay I describe
simply moves away from itself
No anchors! No conscription!
No transactions disguised as traffic!
Ask if there's a castle on the hill
Ask if there's a hill on the hill
Is lettuce on the table still a description?
Ink's ruined everything passes through our papery house
The sun of visual experience passes through our papery house

THREE POEMS
FOR THE END OF THE EARTH

I.

In one version of the culture of signs, raising skyward a rifle removed from its ornamental scabbard is an apology; in another—aggression.

Is there an act that says languagelessly I am speaking this? Shoo the watchmaker from modernity back to his catalogue of myopic antiquation. The orange noise of feathers and bread was digitized decades ago.

Still, the Huns take their hill; the highway, its toll; the hillside, branded with billboards like Baghdad with abstention. It's the "in thing"—this conjugation of hieroglyphics crushed by maternity.

A photographer rubs a doll in soot, tossing it in front of the collapsed apartment complex.

In what I took for the last days of the earth every wound everywhere was eviction.

II.

There's work in Nantucket, savages to the west, a nice lady down that road there that'll earn you a dollar or two but in honest ways, god-fearing ways.

If speech is just ornamental communication, if art is just speaking ornately synonyms for elsewhere, if love and love, then blah blah blah goes the girl down the lane singing of pain, goes the line in the song whose words she sang wrong, go the tropes and the trochees, London Bridge falling down.

Lay clover at the mouse hole, rub butter on the burn, salt over the shoulder, turn three times and spit. The devil may come through a cut if it ain't cleaned right.

In what I took for the last days of the earth every wound everywhere was eviction from tomorrow.

III.

A swan's obedience to the few strokes of ink pinning it flightless to paper exposes our desire to imbue with consciousness not the image but what the image is now forced to assume.

It was the afternoon. There was the bright sky's brilliancy. We were reading about the outdoors, the invention of plastic, text spilling all over the place.

This is the way the world rends.

Before the grammatical "you" was the second person, it was the first to arrive, aimlessly kicking up dirt, hitching a ride to the nearest rail yard.

What is work if not the appearance of purpose given its reward? if not like a cloud in your eye, a thimble of gin, a tiny thread, and the mouth smaller still sewn up.

How to say what I took for the last days of the earth, what I took from the last days of the earth, woundless, windowless, so-so comeuppance.

ANOTHER COMMENT ON THE TEXT

(after D. S.)

Out of the evening, ash ate the ground
A mouth of identical substance was deleted and the dress,
      torn to glittering scarves, less carelessly
  randomized.
Four survivors walked out of the Indian
tidal wave.
Earth as clouds, clouds as a corpse
Evening as a victim one fully rendered
In wide white chalk and suturing the darkened center
Of its ownerless outline.

And a leaden skiff leaving us on land
January in July and the Old Testament
Proper nouns: presence.

Performance, pageantry, *coup de grâce.*

Like the dull female peacock near the grey fir

Palpable isolation and palpable intention. Protuberance.
Prisca's grave prelude.
Innocence white Experience glossy red Songs are always green
I shun you in reach
I find you in distance
Your mask like a forest painted on both sides of the stage

AN OLDER VERSION OF EMERGENCE

Improbable for a tear to dissolve
On the laminated page, but it does so
This is the great contradiction of joy
It moves by exception
For which there are no models
Save pottery fragments in plexiglass
Suspended by pins
Clumps of pollen
Drifting like cloud refuse
Through the interior
Of the obvious simile
The pleasant day
Resists parsing
But tragedy too discloses
Deleting provocation
Dressed in a paradox of renaissance drag
Through silence the utopia cries aloud
Remove vegetation
To achieve historical authenticity
No anchors
No conscription

No transactions done by dint of continual falling
And not a verb
Noise like weeds a judgment
And not a category
There is only one story: disruption
Another neorealist line on the abstract canvas
Of the earth, no bigger
Than a fingernail, no bigger
In the distance, another distance
Another animal moving across November
Another mark on paper
A huge prominence pulls away from the sun
Decorative motifs pouring forth like doctrine
The ionosphere is a grid
The cricket's ankle impenetrable
The moon wedged between
Two victims of fully embodied rhetoric
Two bodies in a small airplane circling Iceland
Forget Icarus
Forget Daedalus
Stop all the downloading
There is a stork inside my stillness
Dance and therapy identical to a trail
Of bread crumbs leading out of the scorched cliché
Where revolution makes Russian tea French
And there is no tree, no modernism

No mark to indicate where the actors stop
No mention of swans
No trace and no difference
Nothing permanently attached to a pencil
The first eraser was a hunk of bread
Hunger, an agent of fertility
Loud as a photograph of lightning
And like a late Turner with no outline
Ineradicable
Is it our lot to be among the living
As portraiture
Are purple flowers scattered
At your feet exaltations of an endless death
Austere extravagance
Decorated like a good nurse
To show love
Opening a chasm in the ground
Really was abstinent
Anyone freed from the tyranny of fact
Can construct the perfect building
Vallejo lived inside earthquakes
Trakl painted crows on his sister's dress
What image merits an afternoon
In which our idleness expands
One sky with the idea of another
Only to be deflated

By a gull pushing through it
Pragmatic as the five-legged ant
Fleeing Muslim persecution to settle in Egypt
All of our sunny anecdotes are allegorical
All stations steal the news from each other
If silence is the major ceremony among the living
For whom at death sweetest music remains
Then it's not the beauty of backwardness
But the backwardness of beauty
That decorates us in transitory certainty
Compelling microtonal change
Whomever shouts loudest
Knows accompaniment far less than melody
And like snow making visible a spider's web
This devouring happiness is living infectiously
Add to the picture an angular stroke
And artificiality trumps again
The definition of the word *design*
While in silk the spider barricades herself
Extending two pedipalps
Which suggest the single couplet
To survive the Sapphic present
Beauty endures as long as there's a looker
But goodness always looks beautiful
I look at you as an aerial trip over paradise
At the cellular level

Spinning and weaving in extreme fragility
A dialectic of emergence
You can spring fully armed
From the head of your father
Or as a larva eat through the leaf
On which your egg was lain
Either way, a latent sexual content
Removes drama from the earth
Shalom, goodnight, adieu
The stone is ripped from the statue
And an animal sings
In hurried inversions
Without its horn
Shalom, goodnight, adieu
Impossibly the tear soaks through

AGAINST ERASURE

Tinkering with trace elements
or punching holes
to pry the copper piping
from your mother's insect voice
either way you'll wake up in static
which is like falling asleep in snow
Call it a tiny treasure
surrounded by a summer horse
& admit that there's a cup of coffee
inside every meaningful thing
you've ever said

The green corn gleams

—Wallace Stevens

4

SCORCHED ANECDOTE

What begins
an accrual
of weak electric
impulses
ends

as scales
practiced
on the library steps

Notes rise. Days rise
I rise, then summer rises

The carpenter bee
understands nothing
of helicopters

The helicopter pilot
understands bees
perfectly

Salvage
from declaratives
vulnerability

Salvage
Monica
from Travis
& summer from me

Lettuce on paper,
blackberry juice on the words:
"we're this & we're that aren't we?"

PEDAGOGICAL IMPERATIVE

True, sunlight was, for a time,
nomadic, if only in our affectionate
rejection of actually having to give it
a name. The more we thought
about it, the more the thought
would recede, condensing elsewhere
and later on. A candle doesn't care
about shadows, nor should it,
waiting to leave less of itself
in the same way. But which way was it?
All this talk of illumination and already
the under-lit hallway of self-composure
seems ready to erupt, or, more accurately,
to collapse, although they're both
insufferable stand-ins for what we were
after—non-picturesque separation,
like stepping purposefully in a puddle
to become saturated with whatever
the world's put in front of you.
And behind? We don't look that way
anymore, do we? The door faces only
ever-outward permanence, until that
too, friends, dim constellations, fades.

A NEW KIND OF POEM

for Arda Collins

There is no ocean
in your ear
to it.

What there is
is this
muffin, left a long time
on the granite countertop.

It is a kind of decision.

You decide to write a new poem.

Invent a better equipped kitchen.

Stainless steel appliances, a refrigerator
whose refusal to hum
is both frightening and reconciliatory.

It gets quieter. It gets sort of orange.

You think of the word *lavender*.

You have no choice but to.
There it is, just floating
direly in front of your face.

How many types of ambiguity
can a muffin conjure up?

Did you really ask yourself this?

Between the questions, as between
two towering beachfront hotels,
there are waves upon waves
upon waves passing through
a tiny sliver of ocean.

What, exactly, do you think
of the word *lavender*?

Do you think you can put your ear to it?

I'm trying to be completely unambiguous.

If I were to say, "The only thing inside a muffin
is muffin," I would certainly mean it.

THE LAUGHING ALPHABET

A FACT CUTS ITSELF IN TWO on the landing below the *Book of Dreams*. Becomes part flowering muscle, half a piece standing in for the Queen. But what of the magistrate, up in arms & waving from the margins where there is endless commerce & an amaranth on the sill? & the window itself? Its hypotheses & electronics? The white wires will stand for science, lines in the author's poker face taken on faith. Betraying the historical underpinnings, a pin pulled outside of Alexandria.

HOW MANY WAYS can one conjugate the word *cargo*, asks the genius in the light bulb. Asks the thorn in the sentence's foot that is not grammar but the poem turning inward, tearing along an infinite plane of current. A cue to place the pencil down & wait for the refrain to repeat itself: muted hieroglyphics, mud tracked from the Woman of Many Dinner Guests & the history of meals past horrid-eyed prison ships & the holding of radiation.

I'M WRITING WITH MY ARMS RAISED. A lion noise at the burning of the library that is not Courage saying: look at my thin wrists, a particular curtain in a certain light, an illustration of the uninformed child, the fool, the wicked man & the sage. One's wearing the Laughing Alphabet. One's singing to a blue fox at forest's edge. One chews his pencil to gray mush. One grinds her thumbs to powder. & the view from the window—a smaller window, someone staring out.

THOUGH YOU IMAGINE A PERPETUAL FLAME only to collect ash from a wooden spoon, this is neither an allegory nor a click track taken out of the final cut. A rocking chair on the Isle of Small Wonders stands for itself. An instantaneous account of purported events for solvent history. A jacket that may or may not establish dignity when the hour flickers out. But enough swaying back & forth. There is the lateness of a buried river to attend to, a photograph of its misshapen bed.

TELEPROMPTERS SPIRAL to an undescendible stair. The curtain coming down as a single point of light in the center of the screen, a perpetual exit to a staged response painted on the backdrop the sun flares into. I was born at 1515 Echo Lane. Such was life in the house of latent immobility, Night-ness & Day-ness an indifference to public affairs. Inside, the argument made more heat than light. & upstream, water & green rocks, glistening bells whose hands like hooks hover a moment & release their catch.

AT THE EMPTY HOUSE on an endless runway, a landing overlooks the possibility of birds & the forest goes blue with ice. Remember the bullet's marked decomposition, the general, the infantry, endless amounts of iron? A generalization beginning with the half-life one asks of age? The lace bug & the ash-gray leaf bug, the ambush bug & the assassin bug, the water scorpion & the European earwig, the true katydid, the Jerusalem cricket asking, asking where will I put my money when they come to re-panel the walls?

THE FOOL WORKED MORNINGS on his forgery, a blue crayon & a voice played back on a handheld recorder, its regional drawl recounting a dream of the other nothing. One sets time against itself & the key fits but it won't turn to the left or the right but it fits & that makes you happy if only for a few seconds. There were plastic bags in the highest branches. Ribbons of smoke above the river. A house on the hill stretching its wax wings. Was it a consolation prize or purely original silence?

A FACT CUTS ITSELF IN TWO on the landing
From an abstract intimacy comes a stunted acceleration
One dragonfly empting itself into another mid-flight
& I play a warden in flowered dress

YAR'S REVENGE

for Graham Foust

What is technology if not

a kind of built-in nostalgia

for the frantic past's long slide

into a slower present

Put another way: a decade

bends 8-bit bells & whistles

into an oxymoron it nearly

hurts remembering

tight lump on your thigh

of quarters in those short

short shorts. It was amazing

when we could bring it home

Now, it's amazing when we can't

BEST AMERICAN
EXPERIMENTAL POETRY

If you turn
your head
this way, like
this, to this
exact point, this
one here—there,
right there, that
point there, if you
turn your head
there, to that
angle, that one,
if your head's
precisely
like this—right
here, exactly
here, if
you turn
your head
there, then
you feel
a sudden
sharp pain
run through
your entire body.

All day long
you continue
to test
the correctness
of this cause
and effect; and
all day long
the results
are the same.
You're enamored
with this, so
much so that
you willingly
subject yourself
again and again
to the pain
in order to
experience
the rare
simplicity
of a proposition
so easily confirmed

SUMMER IN WINTER IN SUMMER

The bottom teeth of summer

in winter, braided into

whomever stood on the green green bridge watching her shadow lengthen.

Sun-pocket. Sunflower. Seedling, you

brittle blossoming something the room clears of dailyness.

Daily, the bottom teeth of summer

in winter, chewing through

ropes, raree-show rapunzeled, which is realism

like this that there can be. These are really happened

tell me again stories I will. I will again against it.

Diving bell in a glass of water. Cacti atmosphere.

A perfect piece of pink cake

complicating perfection's tendency to falter.

Who left it on the counter? Who walked through the room

as though through a composition? The speaker enters quietly,

closes a window, clearing dust from the chair

to sit in the center of the poem, invigorated

with inky awkward blankness.

The bottom teeth of summer

in winter chattering: here's the moon. Here's the moon

splashed over two dozen calendars. Here, the kids are grown.

The day is long. The bed, wide as a battleship, waits

in its buoyancy. Imagine a life and live in it. Imagine dead as ever

walking a cut lily back to water. Crazy epic crazier still trying

to put down roots. Summer in winter like a speaker

in water. The loudest electric sound is nothing compared

to the soundest perforation. My paper life. My paper doll.

Your paper boy. Sun sun sunflower seed summer you

can say you love in a poem's inky blank awkwardness

your paper boy. Sun sun sunflower seed summer you

to the soundest perforation. My paper life. My paper doll

in water. The loudest electric sound is nothing compared

to put-down roots. Summer in winter like a speaker

walking a cut lily back to water. Crazy epic crazier still trying

in its buoyancy. Imagine a life and live in it. Imagine dead as ever

the day is long. The bed, wide as a battleship, waits,

splashed over two dozen calendars. Here, the kids are grown

in winter chattering: here's the moon. Here's the moon.

The bottom teeth of summer

with inky awkward blankness

to sit in the center of the poem, invigorated,

closes a window, clearing dust from the chair.

As though through a composition, the speaker enters. Quietly,

who left it on the counter? Who walked through the room

complicating perfection's tendency to falter.

A perfect piece of pink cake.

Diving bell in a glass of water. Cacti atmosphere,

tell me again stories I will I will. Again, against it

like this that there can be. These are really happened

ropes, raree-show rapunzeled. Which is realism

in winter: Chewing through

.

daily the bottom teeth of summer?

Brittle blossoming something the room clears of dailyness?

Sun-pocket. Sunflower. Seedling, you

whomever stood on the green green bridge watching her shadow lengthen

in winter, braided into

the bottom teeth of summer.

THE JOHNS

in collaboration with David Perry

Several hypotheses of municipal experience
collectively render archaic the concept of citizenry.

The other way around leaves one
feeling rather circular. They're so French

they even understand democracy in America.
Calming sunshine, a thin film of dust

on drinking glasses, newly-envisioned carports.
Could one's horn be heard amid the din

of our coerced demurrals? That's your war.
Whodunnit has never been so dull a question.

Now, a car passing our log cabin
obliterates the Wilderness Theory, leaving

in its wake time to consider investing
in that quill pen and inkwell set. You can't

at every circumstantial turn privilege
exchange, hook a few reasonably sized

fish, talk about a bad day to storm
the capital, and expect the American Epiphany

you've been eyeing with such retro-earnestness
to rear its head: action exposes intent; not

to care a straw nourishes the viper
nestled in your lap. One wants to

kick back, relax, and witness unlimited growth
in all directions. Exponentially,

it's about claiming one's legroom. Rugged
individualism—a willingness to give up

the easement. Some of us floozies
actually enjoy the nomenclature.

Is the sensation of doing business
with a stream of disembodied voices

akin to the intonation of a bored chorus
of thirteen-year-old girls? You realize

you can work backwards, of course?
A set of perfectly measured crutches.

The pitted gravel path to the mailbox.
Nothing else of interest propping up

the novel's opening chapter. Ascending
another hundred feet, the balloon's

luminosity begins to dissipate.
Undeterred, geese continue southward.

THE COMPASS

He knowingly spread himself across both seats
is it knowingly or purposefully that one might make

of oneself an example upon which this conjecture
also spreads and is purpose worse than knowledge

a position articulated better than one the body simply
orients itself toward and if I'd said accommodates instead

would that lessen the smugness the act suggests
and what if she preferred to stand what if her preference

were the very thing he'd intuited initially the first conjecture
made without commentary the very thing upon which

without witness without any of us the decision rests
but a decision can't do that once it's made only one

for whom room enough has been granted to make it
might decide otherwise knowingly purposefully

without witness without the smugness upon which
our assumptions also rest no matter what direction

the compass is oriented toward its needle always
points north but I'm not talking about the compass

or needles or north I'm talking about intention
that which has no affection for the steadfast loyalty

of fact that which in effect is only ever conjecture
alive as a man unaware that he's sitting in a poem

alive as the woman standing there beside him

FLAG

for Chris Nealon

I flag beneath the tide of where the energy is up there in the trees
returning to the theme of women gathering water in the pleasure
of early speech I flag beneath the speaking water up there returning
to the trees where I flag energy in the tide of returning women
up there in the pleasure trees beneath the theme gathering I
flag where I flag up early in the trees speaking energy there

is no point to this flagging returns energy to flag a tree there
up where I flag the theme in speech gathering flags in trees
I the trees & I the tides flag a returning theme there in the I
beneath the flag I energize a theme in tides & trees of pleasure
with what flag the energy of gathering a return to the women
in turn I flag where speech is a tree beneath the trees returning

to flags a theme of where energy gathers up in the water returning
women to speech & the pleasure of early speaking in water there
is a flag I do to energy returning themes of trees gathering women
early in the tide up where I flag beneath the water in women trees
is not a pleasure for flags nor a pleasure for I but in speaking pleasure
I flag again to return themes of early flags in energy & in tides there I

gather the water beneath the water returning the flags turning the I
in turn toward early speech of trees & pleasure where the returning
flag is up in the theme of trees gathered by energy returning pleasure
to early women & themes of speech in the tide where trees there
return to early flags I speak to the women gathering a return to trees
in theme & flags in water & tides up where the early energy of women

is a flag I turn beneath trees to themes of early tides & early women
beneath I flag the theme I flag & flag the trees I flag & flag the water I
flag beneath & flag the energy I flag & flag the returning flag of trees
I flag early & flag up & flag beneath & flag toward the trees returning
the flags beneath the energy in flags & trees & water & speech & there
is no pleasure to flag I flag no pleasure no flags up where the pleasure

is not I flag up early beneath pleasure I flag pleasure & pleasure pleasure
returning trees to flags to up the energy beneath flags & trees to women
returning energy to flags & flags returning women to the water up there
in the trees & the tides I flag themes of flagging & themes of pleasure I
flag returns up beneath tides in trees & tides in flags & tides returning
to the theme of returning I flag speaking in trees & energy & water in trees

flagging an early flag I flag the returning tides of trees & the pleasure
of tides returning women up in trees & flags beneath the returned women
up there where the energy there is a flag I flag to pleasure the returning

AN ACOUSTIC EXPERIENCE

for David Shapiro

Inoculate with ones & zeros
the sound of the human voice

torn in half, tacked to a pixilated heart—
a computer's unrequited compassion

The perfect companion's a photograph of sand

Unexpanding, elegant universe
something something something the end

this poem has been removed for further study

—Tom Raworth, "University Days"

5

THIS

This guardrail

This bluishness

This potato

This suchness

This garlic

This tangency

This pickle

This gray, gold knife's serrations

This egg (and that egg) and their difference (outwardly minimal)

This confusion over maps

This wooden figurine (a fisherman)

This song ringing in so-and-so's head

This Armenian

This word (procrustean)

This poem:

    "Chips"

      Doritos
      Cheetos
      Madhouse Munchies
      Lay's
      Tostitos
      Erik Estrada
      Pringles

This outlook

This exposition

This green(ish) sock

This nonchalant, unfelt condolence

This sadly broken little table I can't bring myself to part with

This slowly approaching sunbeam

This sentence by Marguerite Duras (translated by Barbara Bay):

"Among those watching the scene in the lounge from the road behind the hotel is a man."

This typeface (Century)

The way the light is hitting those trees (This light, I mean)

This (what, concrete?) cat statue

This blue Bic lighter (and that orange one)

This signage

This speculation

This verve

This nickel-and-dime delinquency

This abandoned (until now) stanza:

> Tennyson in collage like Cousteau in Jethro Tull
> and Teresa of Ávila in a libretto by Gertrude Stein
> Tennyson in collage like Twilight in college
> and thousands of Alexanders asserting greatness
> above the bathroom sink.

This predaciousness

This selection of 50 famous quotations

This lack of a microwave (use the oven)

This wineglass-shouldered wife

This accounting for one's times

This suspect motive

This radio-controlled car

This letter from David Markson

This grivance (without an "e")

This purview

This piece of chocolate

This hunger pang (which I'm trying to ignore)

This difficulty

This dumpling (a literal one, not the term of endearment)

This odd, blackened branch

This poem:

> That silence—
> the one both
> state of being
> and command
> insists we bring
> the other kind
> with us. Think
> of a closed mic.
> *There, there*
> that's enough
> thinking.

This warmth (from that sunbeam)

This bleach

This echo

This tomato

This teahouse

This streak of luck

This transparency

This expressiveness

This gnat

This gnat (not the same one)

This hesitation

This grievance (with an "e")

This extra spac e

This, what's the word for it?—frankness?—aggression?—will

This crystal on the desk (and that book about a different one)

This porch

This planter

This rhythmic pacing

This drawstring

This sandbag

This incalculable pleasure (as in the option to stare at the stage or the lights illuminating it—all those bugs intoxicated by brightness)

So the song ringing in so-and-so's head

This glistening wedge of lemon

This exchange (with a stranger on a bus in Denver)

> "Shanghai, Bangkok, or Hong Kong? I'll let you decide."
> "I don't understand the question."
> "Where's she from."
> "How do you know she's not from New Jersey?"

This buildup

This accrual

This litany

This anaphora

This momentum

This yellow jacket (the garment)

Walt Whitman, William Blake, etc.

Sylvia Plath, Emily Dickinson, etc.

So that song ringing in so-and-so's head

I am not available

I am not available to chat

I am obliged to abandon bird algebra's blue government of blueness

I take this obligation seriously

Then I set it down with care

Walt Whitman, William Blake, etc.

This summation

This spackle really covers the contours of the kitchen ceiling

This emoticon really expresses the truth of what I'm feeling

This that could be that

Now we're getting somewhere

This could point to anything

This could be either an autonomous aphorism or the phrase to follow:

one motion speaks to the next in utter clarity without the confines of language

It's like a poem, Mr. So-and-So, these lines ringing in my head.

These lines and what they said

But abstractions stapled to the earth

But display cases and dart boards

But the fire of distant cities visible even now through this thick fog

Gérard de Nerval, Abraham Lincoln, etc.

I have five kinds of machismo I can climb out of

I want to say it again

This time in a smaller font

I have five kinds of machismo I can climb out of

That didn't work

I want to say it again

This time in a smaller font

I have five kinds of machismo I can climb out of

There, steady now

These three paragraphs:

1.

What struck me first was the odd conclusion that, although it's abstract, I was nonetheless looking at a narrative painting, by which I mean that the work includes the manipulation of time. Although the painting is dominated by intersecting lines and shapes in multiple colors, its real subject is the collision of these constituent elements into a system of directives. Thus, the work becomes wedded to duration. One is sent chaotically all over the canvas, searching for the origin or endpoint of the various, mazelike lines, as they connect and intersect, while jettisoning one monochromatic color for another. There is the continually thwarted sense that one might actually reach either an end or a beginning, but, of course, this never occurs.

2.

Although it's never certain where things take place, or to whom those things are happening, her work does evoke a sort of intellectual voyeurism. One is made privy to the infesting of otherwise innocuous objects and gestures with meaning that often feels grotesque, sinister, or at the very least, shameful. The tension is so palpable in that one feels as though one has opened a door onto an indiscriminately compromised scene; however, and this is her real strength, as such a scene is always slightly out of focus, it is the feeling, rather than the event, that takes precedence, leaving one awash in the attendant emotion of witnessing what one probably shouldn't have.

3.

He is reading from an unpublished novel. The room is packed. Maybe it wasn't packed, I don't remember looking around. I was transfixed by the pages themselves, the way he'd let them float to the floor once he'd finished with each. Falling, their quiet descent softened the aggressive enthusiasm behind the gesture of allowing them to do so. They looked like tiny ghosts. They looked like dresses.

Walt Whitman, William Blake, etc.

This perfectly balanced plain jack-in-the-box psychosis

This I-think-I-can engine riding an otherwise mimetic account

This ending:

Poems shouldn't make you wait for them to finish.
Like love, they should finish making you wait.

& this one:

Goodnight motherfucking moon, goodnight

When I said *Something Something Something the end*
I'm pretty sure I meant it

Afterword

At recess in the sixth grade, I am a celebrity. I tell my classmates stories about myself, articulate the daring and exciting delinquency of my past. With each story, my celebrity grows. Soon, I've told them everything. I have no more stories. I am ignored on the playground, and so begin acting out again. This alienates me even more from my classmates, who come to resent my brutishness, to see it as a virus, which, fearful of infection, they avoid whenever possible. In *The Theater and Its Double*, Artaud begins with a lengthy analogy between the plague as a psychic entity whose contagion might be a matter of will and the theater as a sort of disease that carries a potential simultaneously destructive and redemptive. Because of my classmates' preference for stories over the participation—even the passive, observational participation—required of witness, the theater of actual events, my celebrity, was willfully deflated, cast aside, allowed to curdle into something dangerous, something unapproachable. Something adult. This something was itself a kind of theater, the kind which, as Artaud notes, "causes the mask to fall, reveals the lie, the slackness, baseness, and hypocrisy of our world." If, as Joan Didion famously wrote, "[w]e tell ourselves stories in order to live," then what happens when we've told them all, when we run out of these stories, when we have to live in order to tell them? This is the point where the chatter and babble of the adult world suddenly becomes intelligible. This is where the poem begins: the Word Kingdom. When I was about twenty, I remember sitting in my room one night, annoyed with something my housemates were up to, and a bit bored with whatever my other friends were doing. It was one of those evening where you just feel aimless, off-balance, agitated. There was something gnawing at me, but I didn't know what. Then, out of nowhere, a procession of sirens passed by my house. I mean there were fire trucks, police cars, a few ambulances, lots and lots of noise—sudden, alarming noise; then, nothing. It was dead silent for maybe a second or two before the sirens picked up again. This time they seemed to come from every direction, as though they were surrounding the house. But the pitch was off, all wobbly, a weird vibrato, like electronics trying to run on nearly dead batteries. The sound wasn't coming from the sirens at all. It was an animal sound. It was every dog in the neighborhood at once attempting to imitate the noise. It was the word *kingdom*. None of them could do it quite right, but damn were they going for it. It felt simultaneously sad and triumphant. It was the exact moment I decided to be a writer. I'm not writing the noise of the sirens, nor am I writing the noise of the dogs. I hope my poems take root in the silence after the two have sounded: mimetic chatter and babble moving paradoxically from intellection to imagination. The word *kingdom* in the Word Kingdom.

Acknowledgments

Grateful acknowledgment is made to the editors of the following journals in which excerpted versions of this work first appeared: Academy of American Poets' Poem-A-Day email campaign, *Big Game Review*, *Blackbox Manifold*, *Boston Review*, *The Brooklyn Rail*, *Columbia Poetry Review*, *Double Room*, *Eleven Eleven*, *English Language Notes*, *Front Porch Journal*, *Ink Node*, *Interrupter*, *Many Mountains Moving*, *Massachusetts Review*, *The Modern Review*, *Narrative*, *New American Writing*, *Omniverse*, *Parthenon West Review*, *Phoebe*, *Real Poetik*, *Sentence*, *Versal*, *Volt*, *Washington Square*, *Web Conjunctions*, *Weird Deer*, *Zing Magazine*.

Poems from this book also appeared in the following anthologies: *The Volta Book of Poets* (Sidebrow, 2014), *The Force of What's Possible: Writers on Accessibility & the Avant-Garde* (Nightboat Books, 2014), *Villanelles* (Everyman's Library, 2012), *Zoland Poetry* (Zoland Books, 2009), and *The Bedside Guide to No Tell Motel* (No Tell Books, 2006).

"Yar's Revenge" appeared in the Fact-Simile Editions Poetry Trading Card Series. "What Do I Know" appeared in the 2013 Best of the Net anthology from Sundress Publications. "Historical Criticism and the Image of the Heart" appeared as a broadside from Squircle Line Press. "Eight Meditations on Enormity, Petrifaction, and Work" was commissioned for the *Manual Labors* exhibit at The Laboratory of Art and Ideas at Belmar, by curator Jake Adam York, in response to a mano discovered in the Four Corners region. "Palatial is the Compass..." was commissioned for the *Call and Response* exhibition at the University of Massachusetts Amherst Main Gallery by curator Diana Simard; it appeared along with a video installation by Marcus DeMaio, both of which were later displayed in *OnandOnScreen*. "Flag" was unintentionally commissioned by Christopher Nealon, whose poem "Three Cinnabar Fields," from *The Joyous Age*, contains the following lines: "Write a poem called Flag/ Write a poem that starts I flag beneath the tide of where the energy is up there in the trees." "Pedagogical Imperative" was commissioned under a different title by G.C. Waldrep for his Yurt Master project. "Summer in Winter in Summer" owes a formal debt to Peter Gizzi's "Vincent, Homesick for the Land of Pictures." Section five of "Ten Way to Take an Airplane Apart" owes a debt to "Someone Puts Together a Pineapple" by Wallace Stevens. The title of the poem "Luggage Arrives in the World Where It Waits" was stolen from Oren Silverman. The source text for "Another Comment on the Text" is David Shapiro's "Commentary Text Commentary Text Commentary Text."

Portions of this book appeared in a chapbook published by The Unwin-Dunraven Literary Ecclesia, a pamphlet published in conjunction with the New Lakes reading series in Missoula, Montana, and in the chapbook *Acoustic Experience*, published by Pavement Saw Press. These poems were composed and revised variously between 2000 and 2013. My deep thanks to everyone at BAP, especially Joe Pan for his continued vision and dedication to the art, and to all the writers around Colorado's Front Range. Thanks to SRM for the eagle eyes.

About the Author

Noah Eli Gordon was born in Cleveland, OH, in 1975, and grew up there and in South Florida, then moved to Boston where he sold jewelry from a cart for several years while attending Bunker Hill Community College, followed by UMass-Amherst, eventually graduating from their Program for Poets & Writers, before moving west and settling in Denver, CO.

His recent books include *The Year of the Rooster* (Ahsahta Press, 2013), *The Source* (Futurepoem Books, 2011), and *Novel Pictorial Noise* (Harper Perennial, 2007), which was selected by John Ashbery for the National Poetry Series and subsequently chosen for the San Francisco State Poetry Center Book Award. His work has appeared in numerous anthologies, including *The Volta Book of Poets* (Sidebrow, 2014), *The Force of What's Possible: Writers on Accessibility & the Avant-Garde* (Nightboat Books, 2014), *Villanelles* (Everyman's Library, 2012), *Postmodern American Poetry: A Norton Anthology 2nd Edition* (W.W. Norton, 2012), *A Broken Thing: Poets on the Line* (University of Iowa Press, 2011), *Against Expression: An Anthology of Conceptual Writing* (Northwestern University Press, 2011), and *Poets on Teaching* (University of Iowa Press, 2010), and was short-listed in *The 2010 Best American Nonrequired Reading*.

An advocate of small press culture, he co-founded (with Joshua Marie Wilkinson) Letter Machine Editions, penned a column for five years on chapbooks for *Rain Taxi: Review of Books*, ran Braincase Press, was Head Reviews editor for *The Volta*, co-founded the little magazine *Baffling Combustions*, and has published numerous reviews, interviews, and critical and journalistic writing. Currently, he teaches courses on poetry, poetics, publishing, and nonfiction for the MFA program in creative writing at the University of Colorado at Boulder, where he directs Subito Press.